# THE GENIUS OF FATHER BROWNE

# THE GENIUS OF FATHER BROWNE

Ireland's Photographic Discovery

E. E. O'Donnell sj

WOLFHOUND PRESS

Published in Great Britain 1991
First published in Ireland 1990 by
WOLFHOUND PRESS
68 Mountjoy Square,
Dublin 1.

British Library Cataloguing in Publication Data
Browne, Francis
    The genius of Fr. Browne: Ireland's photographic discovery
    1.   Irish photographs. Special subjects: Ireland
    I.   Title II.   O'Donnell, E. E.
    779.99415

    ISBN 0-86327-265-7

Profits made by the Jesuit Order from the sale of Fr. Browne's books and prints go to the Jesuit Solidarity Fund recently established to help counteract Ireland's serious unemployment problems both north and south of the border.

Book and cover design: Jan de Fouw. Cover photographs: *Front*, 'The Happy Warrior' — John Boohan of Kilbeggan (1929) and detail from 'In the shadow of the Press' at Longford (1935); *Back*, At Aston's Quay (1945). See pages 44, 67 and 75. Photographic prints by David H. Davison, Pieterse-Davison International Ltd., Dublin. Duotone separations: Colour Repro Ltd., Dublin. Typesetting and layout: Redsetter Ltd., Dublin. Printed by Betaprint International Ltd., Dublin.

# CONTENTS

*Continued overleaf*

# INDEX of Names and Places

The photographer (left) in the uniform of Chaplain
to the Irish Guards with Fr. Joseph Scannell at Arras
(1918). See page 10.

Deciding on how to arrange the pictures throughout this book was a major testing point for both publisher and myself. In my earlier volume, *Fr. Browne's Ireland: Remarkable Images of People and Places*, I had selected and arranged the photographs on a simple county-by-county basis, a significant objective being to establish the full geographical range of the Irish photographs and to enable readers more readily to identify with the subjects. Since the 'shiring of Ireland' in 1579, counties have become important to Irish ways of thinking; allegiances to our counties are incredibly strong and have ever been a focal point for our emigrants abroad and our social and sporting activities at home. Counties form our more benign political boundaries.

However, it seemed worth changing the principles of presentation this time. The first source remains unchanged: there *are* pictures here from every county. However, we have arranged their sequence somewhat differently. Instead of taking the strictly provincial structure, we have located each photograph in its appropriate place in one of four sections in the book. The rationale for each section is simple: North, South, East or West of Ireland. But within each section the relevant photographs are arranged in a visually determined sequence. The reason for this is to make the picture itself, and not its place of origin, the deciding factor in the choice of position, size and sequence. For photographers and those with a strong visual sense, this is perhaps a rudimentary decision. However, I suspect that for many a general reader without formal training in the 'reading' of visual imagery, the issue of presentation would tend to be a very secondary concern. And certainly, visual sequencing played a secondary role to county of origin in the arrangement established in *Fr. Browne's Ireland*. I hope that this change, together with the additional element of commentary on specific photographs, will help to further enhance the status of the photographer's work.

Fr. Browne's greatness as a photographer is revealed not alone by techniques and compositional skills, but also by the astonishing range and depth of his interests — from new images of traditional Ireland he sweeps effortlessly to the unusual and memorable moments that capture the reality of his time as no other photographer in Ireland has done. We instantly recognise his work as original and true.

This new collection includes a comprehensive range of town and countryside portraits. Col. and Mrs. Plunkett on their elegant staircase are suitably complemented by a game poacher with his illicit catch; the contemplative fisherman by his boat; a most elegant lady in County Cork, wearing the traditional hooded cloak; an Aran Island weaver at Onaght, his loom as companion to his bed; a genuine tinker mending his pots and pans by the roadside; coal deliveries on Ormeau Road, Belfast; 'Dry goods' being transported in Donegal; a Belturbet locomotive in 1938; ploughing at Maguire's Bridge; Dodgems from Ardee in 1936; the President of Ireland in 1948; 'self undergoing anaesthetic' and an appendectomy from 1933: all revealing and thought-provoking pictures that distil the essence of a changing Ireland from 1920 to 1950.

Many of the world's great photographers specialise in portraiture. Others capture the world in action, unplanned movements recognised for their relevance by the trained professional eye of the creative photographer. Fr. Browne blends both with outstanding success. He makes the composed and carefully staged seem casual and spontaneous; he makes of the unexpected moment a timeless, eloquent composition. He was a man of extraordinary energy and had total commitment to the importance of what he was creating in his photography.

I have selected nineteen pictures from this volume for brief commentary. As I researched the negatives, I found that certain images kept returning to my mind — the outstanding glimpse into the life of a travelling family at Urlar, County Mayo in 1930; the body of the dead boy, Eric, in Cappagh mortuary chapel; the sombre faces at a wedding on Aran; the remarkable expressions in several of the close-up portraits of men and women; children window-shopping in Galway; Old Blarney Street in Cork (and a matching street of wind-blown clothes-lines in Limerick); the ferry boat at Lough Erne; 'The Happy Warrior' (also reproduced on the cover), and so on. Seeing these pictures in their social and historical contexts, I have made some technical comments on the photographer's expertise — not in any complete sense, yet hoping through words to win for the picture the reader's closer attention. I have suggested some ways of seeing what Fr. Browne was really doing in his photography.

For the photographer, of course, the photograph *is* the message, the photograph is his statement. We are fortunate in having here a truly great photographer who depicted for and for generations to come, the changing Ireland that he saw through his camera's lens for sixty years.

Fr. Browne did not live to see his negatives in print. He died leaving to his Jesuit Order this legacy of photographic jewels taken in twenty-eight different countries. Full recognition of his great talent and achievement is in its early stages. The publication of *Fr. Browne's Ireland* and the sponsorship by Allied Irish Bank of the preservation of the negatives have provided two important stages for what is now a clear groundswell of international interest.

When he died in 1960, Father Browne left 42,000 negatives behind him. Unfortunately, the majority of these are on unstable, nitrate-based film which is rapidly deteriorating and not expected to survive the turn of the century. Some of the early photographs are already badly disfigured. An example is given here. It shows Father Browne in the uniform of Chaplain to the Irish Guards standing with Father Joseph Scannell in the ruins of Arras Cathedral in 1918. (Joseph Scannell, incidentally, was another Corkman. He became one of the city's most eminent priests. He was the first Chaplain to the Forces of the Irish Free State and later became President of St Finbarr's College, Farranferris, Parish Priest and Dean of Cork. Monsignor Scannell died in 1961.) The frontispiece of this book shows a portion of the same Arras photograph with the blotches removed.

Before any further deterioration of the negatives occurred, I was particularly happy that Allied Irish Bank agreed to sponsor the conservation of the Collection, an operation costing many thousands of pounds. The Irish Jesuits are most appreciative of this generous and far-sighted intervention on the part of AIB.

The conservation work itself is proceeding quickly. It involves transferring the negatives to safety-film, a complicated process, and simultaneously indexing them by computer. Some of the very early negatives that were saved last year have already disintegrated beyond redemption: the images have simply disappeared. The good news is that nothing has been lost. David Davison, the member of the Irish Professional Conservators and Restorers Association who is doing the work, has managed to save even the negatives that were in worst condition. It was David Davison, too, who made the prints for this book. I am most grateful to him and to Seamus Cashman of Wolfhound Press for all their help.

E. E. O'Donnell S.J.
Gonzaga College,
Dublin 6.

# BIOGRAPHICAL NOTES

1880 Francis Mary Hegarty Browne, born in Cork, Ireland. Grandson of James Hegarty, Lord Mayor of Cork.

1897 Toured Europe with his brother and his camera. Took photographs of France, Italy, Switzerland. Joined the Jesuits.

1899-1902 Attended Royal University Dublin. Contemporary of James Joyce. Took First Class Honours in Classics.

1903-1906 Philosophy studies at Chieri, N. Italy. Photographed Venice, Monte Carlo etc.

1906-1911 Teacher at Belvedere College, Dublin. Founder Editor of *The Belvederian*. Founder of the Camera Club.

1909 To Rome by sea, via Lisbon. Photograph of Pope (now Saint) Pius X. Visited Naples and Pompeii.

1911-1916 Theology studies at Milltown Park, Dublin.

1912 Sailed on RMS *Titanic*, Southampton-Cherbourg-Queenstown. Memorable photographs published in *Daily Sketch* after disaster, including last photo ever taken of Captain Smith and only photo ever taken in Marconi Room.

1915 Ordained a priest by his uncle, Robert Browne, Bishop of Cloyne.

1916-1919 Chaplain to the Irish Guards in France, Belgium and Germany. Wounded five times. Frequently mentioned in dispatches. Won Military Cross and Bar and Croix de Guerre. Described by General (later Field Marshall, Lord) Alexander as 'the bravest man I ever met'. Photographs of Belgium, Holland, 'The Watch on the Rhine', etc.

1920-1923 Teacher at Belvedere College, Dublin. (His collection has 4,600 photographs of Dublin).

1924-1925 Australia (900 photographs, including all major cities). Went out via Capetown; returned via Cocos Islands, Ceylon, Saudi Arabia, Aden, Suez Canal, Egypt, Crete, Salonika, Naples, Toulon, Gibraltar, Spain and Portugal.

1926-1928 Superior, St. Francis Xavier's Church, Gardiner Street, Dublin.

1929-1960 Member of Jesuit Mission Staff — giving parish retreats throughout Ireland and UK. Contributed photographic essays to *The Kodak Magazine* and many other periodicals. Photographed the churches of East Anglia (for the Church of England Church Governing Body) and English prehistoric sites (for the British Museum). Took over 3,000 photographs of England, Scotland and Wales.

1960 Died in Dublin, where he was visited on his death-bed by Lord Alexander.

1985 Father Browne's 42,000 negatives were discovered in a trunk in the Jesuit Archives, Dublin.

1987 Browne photographs were used to illustrate *The Annals of Dublin* by E. E. O'Donnell SJ, published by Wolfhound Press who commissioned the volume, *Fr Browne's Ireland*.

1988 Conservation of the Browne Collection begun, sponsored by Allied Irish Bank.

1989 Publication of *Father Browne's Ireland* by Wolfhound Press. Two major features on the Collection published in the London *Independent*.

1990 First public exhibition of Father Browne's photographs presented by AIB at St. Margaret's Church of England, Uxbridge, London.

*Tyrone*
*Donegal*
*Derry*
*Fermanagh*
*Belfast*
*Monaghan*
*Cavan*
*Armagh*
*Antrim*
*Down*

In Father Browne's time, the towns and cities of the North were linked by the network of the Great Northern Railway. Apart from the lines that still connect Belfast with Derry, Bangor, Larne and Dublin, this network has now disappeared. Like most non-commuters, Father Browne liked to travel by train. In this chapter we find evidence of the joy he took in locomotion. His Collection, overall, includes hundreds of photographs of railways and railwaymen, some taken as far afield as Laura in Australia and along the banks of the Suez Canal in Saudi Arabia.

Northern Ireland's three cities — Belfast, Derry and Armagh — are represented here, as are some rural parts of the three counties of Ulster — Donegal, Cavan and Monaghan — which are in the Republic of Ireland.

In his own index of his negatives, the photographer had a special section called 'Seasons'. He travelled through the North during all four seasons, so examples of all four are shown here. The winter scenes in Belfast, Antrim and Monaghan are particularly striking. Spring is illustrated by the ploughing scene in County Fermanagh; summer by the buggy-driver near Glaslough House and by the gathering of past-pupils at Thornhill Convent; autumn by the stormy day on Lough Derg in Donegal and the mellow fruitfulness of mushrooms at Cookstown, County Tyrone.

Father Browne was in his early forties when Ireland and Ulster were partitioned. He had many friends — of all persuasions and none — north of the Border and frequently visited them with his camera. The interior of a friend's house in suburban Belfast can be contrasted in this section with the open hearth of a small cabin in the Cavan hills.

*Opposite:*
North Point: Malin Head (1929). County Donegal.

Selling mushrooms to passing motorists,
Cookstown (1930). County Tyrone.

'Dry goods' being loaded by the Inishowen Bus Company in The Diamond at Carndonagh (1929). County Donegal.

Derry City is located on the site of a monastery founded by St. Columb in the year 546. This photograph, taken in 1940, from the roof of St. Columb's College, Bishop Street, shows St. Columb's (Church of Ireland) Cathedral with its spire, and St. Columb's (Catholic) Church — better known as the Long Tower — on the left. County Derry.

*Stanley's Walk, off Lecky Road, where this pump stood, was demolished in the mid 1960s. (1940) County Derry.*

'Depression Personified' would, to my mind, be a good caption for this portrait which was taken in Stanley's Walk, Derry City in 1940. Male unemployment in the city at the time was the highest anywhere in these islands. The women went out to work — mainly in the famous shirt factories — while the menfolk remained at home to mind the children and look after the house.

From personal experience, I know that the little, terraced, two-storey houses off the Lecky Road were kept extremely well. Their owners were heart-broken when the whole district was demolished in the early 1960s to make way for modern houses on an altogether different street-plan. Most of the old houses, it must be admitted, lacked amenities such as running water and indoor toilets. My father's house (106 Bogside — only two blocks from here) was still lit by gaslight until 1955.

The portrait itself is unusual. The lady is posed. The picture is composed. Yet there is something unposed about it — probably due to the dog. You can see, especially from her shoes, that the lady is by no means test a pauper. Her haggard expression, however, conveys a deep sense of gloom. At the same time, there is an undoubted sense of strength, of indefatigability. 'We shall not be moved'. But we were, nonetheless.

Miss McCabe accompanies her daughter Eileen on the harp during a recital at the Reparation Convent in Clones (1954). County Monaghan.

The interior of a house in Derryvolgie Avenue,
Belfast, in 1949. Belfast City.

The coal-man on the Ormeau Road in Belfast (1937).
Belfast City.

*Up to recent times, the Belfast terminus of the Great Northern Railway was at Great Victoria Street. This view of the station was taken in 1938. Belfast City.*

---

Crowd scenes are difficult to photograph, but this one, taken at the terminus of the Great Northern Railway in Belfast in 1938, shows how effective they can be.

The first problem Father Browne had to face here was *where to stand*. To achieve the desired effect, the sense of impatience and crush, he needed to stand as close to the people as possible, while still retaining his distance, in order to record as much detail as he could.

The second problem was one of composition: how could the photographer create order out of chaos? Father Browne 'framed' this picture excellently. He controlled the depth of field and exposure, included everything of importance, paid attention to detail. All the visual elements look right and 'hold together' in a way that gives us a sense of having been present in Great Victoria Street on that day in 1938.

An example of his attention to detail can be seen in the advertisement for the Donegall Square* insurance company, seen in perfect focus. For the photographer, this spelling of Donegal with a double 'l' was synonymous with Belfast. So much so, indeed, that he did not include the name of the city in his own caption.

Because the railway station has now been demolished, this is is a particularly valuable recording of the way things used to be.

*Named after Sir Arthur Chichester, marquess of Donegall, who was Lord Deputy 1604-16. His first grant of Ulster land was in Inishowen, Co. Donegal.

*Shadow of a shunter at Enniskeen, near Carrickmacross (1937). County Monaghan.*

---

Compare this photograph of a train with the one of Cobh Cathedral on page 92 below. It is another good example of how the photographer always had an eye open for the unusual.

Luck had a large part to play in this instance because, if it had not been a snowy day, a far less contrasting shadow would have been thrown. But there was more to it than luck. Father Browne often practised with the use of colour filters and it is likely that he selected the appropriate one here to reduce glare and to enhance contrast.

Another piece of luck was that the wind was blowing in the right direction. This enabled Father Browne to keep his lines parallel, moving out of frame to the right. How different the result would have been if the smoke from the stationary locomotive had been heading straight upwards.

The subject itself, of course, will be of great interest to railway enthusiasts. Amazingly, there is sufficient information in this shot for the experts to be able to tell you that the train is the 7.25 a.m. from Enniskillen to Dundalk, stopping in Inniskeen, County Monaghan, at 8.42 a.m. to allow passengers change for Carrickmacross. This Great Northern Railway network was closed in 1957.

A very old locomotive at Belturbet station in 1938.
County Cavan.

Getting up smoke on the Great Northern Railway at Strabane (1935). The railway-line here, which connected Portadown to Derry, was closed in 1957. County Tyrone.

Goraghwood Station (1941). It was here that the customs inspection was carried out on the Great Northern trains running between Belfast and Dublin. The ticket collector is Mr. Walsh; unfortunately, Fr. Browne did not record the name of the Guard. County Armagh.

A summer reunion of past-pupils of Thornhill
Convent near Derry, in July 1940. County Derry.

*Opposite:*
Crowds leaving St. Patrick's Cathedral in Armagh
City (1934) after one of Father Browne's evening
sermons. County Armagh.

Wintry road conditions
near the village of
Carnlough (1937).
County Antrim.

St. Patrick's grave, Downpatrick (1931).
This granite boulder was placed here in
the graveyard of the Church of Ireland
Cathedral in modern times to mark the
reputed burial place of the saint who died
in A. D. 461 County Down.

'The Long Stone' near Mayobridge
(1931). Stones like these marked the
graves of ancient Celtic heroes. County
Down.

Mr. McCann poses for Father Browne near Ballycastle (1929). County Antrim.

*Opposite:*
Panoramic view of Enniskillen (1932). County Fermanagh.

*A helping hand. Ploughing at Maguire's Bridge (1930). County Fermanagh.*

A true expert in his art, Father Browne was not afraid to break some of the fundamental rules of photography if the subject so warranted. In this picture of a ploughman taken at Maguire's Bridge, County Fermanagh, in 1930, we see two striking examples of how rules are made to be broken.

Rule One is: 'Don't show the subject in the centre of the frame because this reduces interest'. Rule Two is: 'Don't show the horizon half-way up a photograph because this splits the image in two'. Father Browne was well aware of these long-established guidelines and usually observed them. Here he felt there was reason to revolt.

He broke Rule One for several reasons. Had he stood *directly* behind the ploughman, the furrows would have run vertically up the frame and the result would have been off balance. Had he stood further to the left, he would have lost the contrasting textures of the ploughed/unploughed parts of the field. He also knew that the diagonal line, running to the left and right of centre more than compensated for the central position of the subject.

He broke Rule Two for several reasons as well. The ploughman's head, the horses' heads and the trees on the skyline, especially in this *vertical* photograph suffice to integrate the upper half of the picture with the lower half. If he had shown less of the field, again the contrasting textures would have been lost. Had he shown less of the sky, the photograph would have lacked its most striking feature, the harmony of the Big Country.

I might add that the 'helping hand' of the child is a classic example of the photographer's 'trademark'.

*Opposite:*
'Northern Lights' was Fr. Browne's caption for this photograph, taken in the Belfast shipyards in 1937. Queen's Island, where the Harland and Wolff yard is located, was originally called Dargan Island after the Carlow engineer who was responsible for the Lagan Channel in the nineteenth century. Belfast City.

Boatman on the strand at Cushendall (1950). County Antrim.

A turf sled near Newbliss (1929). This is not as primitive as it looks: the wheel had been invented but was inclined to become bogged down in wet conditions. County Monaghan.

*Boys hitching up their pony and trap on Upper Lough Erne (1932). County Fermanagh.*

---

As in Clew Bay, there are said to be 365 islands in Lough Erne, County Fermanagh. Trasna Island, seen in the background here (1932) is still one of the Erne's inhabited islands but it was connected to the mainland by bridge in 1935. This picture captures the essence of a way-of-life that is now a thing of the past. Notice how Father Browne has managed to obtain the desired effect by showing the cart being put back behind the horse: the two travelled separately to the jetty on the ferry. It is interesting to compare this photograph with the one of the children looking into a shop window in Galway. In both cases, the photographer has obviously told his subjects *not* to look at the camera. This simple procedure takes the emphasis off the people and places it elsewhere. It is difficult to say precisely *where* else.

It is easy, on the other hand, to see that it is the picture as a whole that is important, not any one detail of it. Contrast this with the several portraits of people shown in the book, for example with the lady in Derry City or with the group of travellers in County Mayo. In the latter two photographs the people *have* been told to look at the camera: hence the totally different effect.

Upper Lough Erne can be quite stormy betimes. It is rarely without a ripple. The photographer was lucky to have hit on a particularly tranquil day on this occasion because the reflections in the still waters of the lake add greatly to the atmosphere of serenity that pervades this work of art.

A stormy day at Lough Derg (1934). St. Patrick's Purgatory, the place of penitential pilgrimage on Station Island, can be seen in the distance. County Donegal.

'A hearth in the hills' near Cavan Town
(1943). County Cavan.

Miss Barbara Vincent-Jones in her buggy
near Glaslough (1949). County
Monaghan.

A tranquil scene in Kilbroney graveyard, near Rostrevor (1929). County Down.

The F.C.A., a local defence force, forms a guard of honour in Virginia (1943). Dr. Lyons, Bishop of Kilmore, has come to town to confirm the Catholic children. County Cavan.

Fr. Keown at the Premonstratensian monastery, Kilnacrott (1950). County Cavan.

*Dublin*
*Laois*
*Louth*
*Kildare*
*Carlow*
*Kilkenny*
*Offaly*
*Wicklow*
*Meath*
*Wexford*
*Longford*
*Westmeath*

For most of his eighty years Father Browne lived in the city of Dublin (where he was stationed at Belvedere College, Gardiner Street Church and Milltown Park) and at Emo in County Laois (where he was based from 1931 to 1957). As a consequence, the Midlands of Ireland and its eastern seaboard came under his closest photographic scrutiny.

Of his 4,600 Dublin photographs, some 130 were used to illustrate my *Annals of Dublin* (Wolfhound Press, 1987) and a further small selection was presented in *Father Browne's Ireland* (Wolfhound Press, 1989). There is room for only another half-dozen in this section, the implication being that most of the magnificent Dublin pictures have still to see the light of publication. The ones I have chosen here show the breadth of the photographer's vision. Who else, for instance, ever photographed himself under anaesthetic awaiting surgery? Who would have thought of visiting the mortuary chapel of a children's hospital as well as the private study of the President of Ireland?

During his life-time, Father Browne turned thousands of his pictures into glass slides for the use of a 'magic lantern'. Besides showing these himself to various groups and societies around the country, he lent many of them to a Mr. Byrne who ran a mobile cinema which toured throughout the eastern counties. This horse-drawn canvas cinema is shown here. Very primitive by to-day's standards, the tent of Mr. Byrne obviously brought hours of entertainment and instruction to the rural masses.

One photograph in this section calls for special comment. The Uilleann Piper in Tullamore town is recorded playing his unwieldy instrument in a standing position, using a specially-adapted walking-stick by way of support. This is extremely unusual, so rare indeed that it may be quite unique.

*Opposite:*
East Point: Wicklow Castle Head (1934). County Wicklow.

Jock Dornan, employee of Córas Iompair Éireann
(the national transport company) at Aston's Quay
(1945). Many of the provincial buses used to depart
from here. Dublin City.

Workmen ripping up O'Connell Street (1930) — a
practice still in vogue. Dublin City.

Decorations on the occasion of the Eucharistic Congress (1932). Sandyford, County Dublin (page 46). *Above*: Dundrum, County Dublin. *Right*: Main Street, Blackrock, County Dublin.

*The body of a small boy, Eric, in the mortuary of Cappagh Hospital (1928). Fr. Browne was a frequent visitor to the children's hospital at Cappagh. County Dublin.*

In the Browne Collection there are many vigorous photographs of children at play and at work. It comes as no surprise, then, that we find — by way of contrast — this study of a dead child.

The composition of this poignant picture of the body of little Eric in the mortuary chapel of Cappagh Hospital (1928) was carefully thought out. How different it would have been if Father Browne had omitted to show the stained-glass window. I think you will find it interesting to look at this photograph again when you have read what I have to say about the 'Kilkenny Fantasy' (see pages 66 & 74). You will realize, then, that what we have here is virtually two images that give birth to a salutary idea in your mind.

Father Browne often photographed dead people: somehow the word 'corpses' seems singularly inappropriate. Another example can be found in this book where we see the dead Bishop of Cloyne, the photographer's uncle, lying in state. It is interesting to compare these two pictures and see that they have something undefinable in common.

When we look at Eric here, the immediate impression, curiously, is not one of horror or despair. On the contrary, there is an overwhelming sense of peace. We cannot explain *why* God has allowed polio to snuff out the life of an innocent child but we do feel more convinced that there is a hereafter, that the Good Shepherd has gathered another lamb into His fold.

A presbytery in Wicklow Town was destroyed by fire in 1928. Schoolboys helped to fight the flames, filling buckets of water from the leaking hose. See also page 51. County Wicklow.

Seán T. O'Kelly, President of Éire, at his residence, Áras an Uachtaráin, in the Phoenix Park (1948). President O'Kelly served from 1945 to 1959. Dublin City.

Malachi Horan of Ballinascorney at the age of ninety-three (1942). His remarkable memoirs were recorded by Dr. George Little, President of the Old Dublin Society, in *Malachi Horan Remembers*. County Dublin.

A presbytery in Wicklow Town
was destroyed by fire in 1928. See
also page 48. County Wicklow.

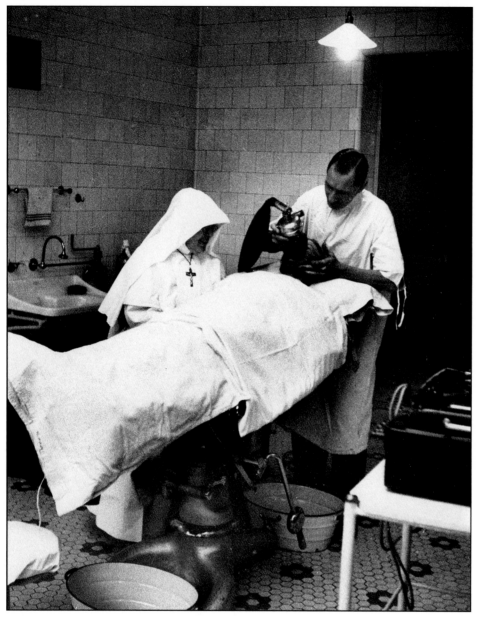

*Opposite:*
The circus comes to Rahan village in 1929. The photographer's comment on the name, 'Corvenieos', was 'alias McCormack's.' County Offaly.

Mr. Byrne's mobile cinema on the Dublin-Cork road near Portlaoise (1942). Many of Father Browne's lantern-slides were shown here. County Laois.

'Self undergoing anaesthetic' is the title of this imaginative photograph taken in St. Vincent's Hospital (1938). In the close-up shot, Mr. Meade is performing an appendectomy. Dublin City.

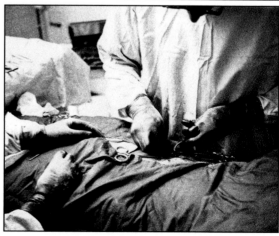

'Hewers of wood' outside Carroll's cigarette factory in Dundalk (1928). County Louth.

*Opposite:*
'Dodgem' cars are the latest craze at the fête for the opening of the new schools in Ardee (1936). County Louth.

Gaelic football at St. Patrick's College, Carlow Town
(1947). County Carlow.

The camogie team at Goresbridge Convent (1952).
Camogie is the feminine form of hurling, a Gaelic
game which dates back to prehistoric times. County
Kilkenny.

'The Piper', Tullamore (1929). The bellows of the Irish bagpipes is inflated by the elbow, not by the mouth. County Offaly.

*Opposite:*
Boys on their way home from school in Tallaght (1925). Dublin City.

Radio-carbon dating shows that the burial-mount at
Newgrange was constructed about 2500 B.C. The
photograph was taken in 1929. County Meath.

*Opposite:*
'The Poacher' at Straffan (1925). County Kildare.

In the saw-mills at New Inn (1933). County Laois.

*Opposite:*
Enjoying the picture page, Longford (1935). County Longford.

Salvaging the wreckage after a railway accident near
Portarlington in 1944. The locomotive belonged to
the Great Southern Railway. County Laois.

Roadside school at Ballinabrannagh (1940). County Carlow.

The wording here took Father Browne's fancy in 1928. County Kilkenny.

*'The Happy Warrior' was how Father Browne described John Boohan of Kilbeggan (1929). County Westmeath.*

Three facets of the photographer's art are well demonstrated in this picture: humour, line and emphasis. 'The Happy Warrior' was Father Browne's humorous caption for his portrait of John Boohan of Kilbeggan (1929). The pose, in itself, is sufficient to convey the sense of fun. It is clear that the photographer knew his subject well and knew how to bring the best out of him.

The diagonal line of the brush-handle is crucial to the success of the shot. It gives a dramatic quality to the photograph that would have been lost had that handle been shown in either a vertical or horizontal line. The straightness of the line is important too: the strength of the image would have been reduced if, say, John had been holding a scythe.

Emphasis has been placed on the *head* of the brush. By keeping it in focus in the foreground, it appears larger than life, grabbing your eye immediately after you have looked at the man's face. In fact the handle of the brush seems to act here as a kind of lightning-conductor, sweeping your glance down, instantaneously, from man's head to brush head. It is interesting to compare this dynamic portrait with the more static one of the Aran weaver (page 112).

*Kilkenny Old and New — a Fantasy' (1932)*

Here we have an example of what film directors call 'montage'. The earliest examples of montage are to be found in the characters of Japanese handwriting that date back to 2650 B.C. For instance, the symbol for a dog combined with the symbol for a mouth gave the word 'bark'. Two concrete symbols, when juxtaposed, gave an abstract meaning.

*See page 74*

In more recent centuries, yet based on the same principle of juxtaposition, the Japanese developed the most laconic form of poetry, the haiku. Consisting of just three lines, the haiku makes two concrete images collide, as it were, in order to burst into the splendour of an abstract effect. The poet Basho provides a good example: A lonely crow / On leafless bough / One autumn eve.

The simple combination of two natural details results, in other words, in a third entity which is qualitatively different: psychologically, the emotions have been reached. The Russian film-director, Sergei Eisenstein, introduced this principle into photography. In a condensed and purified form, he simply juxtaposed two images and allowed the viewers to draw their own (inevitable) conclusions.

My guess is that Father Browne never read Eisenstein's book, *Film Form*, which was not published in English until 1949. Nevertheless, in this 'Kilkenny Fantasy' he fulfilled Eisenstein's prescription to the letter. *How* he produced the double exposure is open to conjecture.

The mower returning from a day's work on the harvest at Ballykilmurray (1929). County Offaly.

*Opposite:*
An elegant old lady at Gorey (1933). County Wexford.

Main Street, Mullingar (1941). County
Westmeath.

Mrs. Frank Lillis with her daughter Mary in
their phaeton at Blackrock (1944). County
Dublin.

*Opposite:*
Col. & Mrs. Randal Plunkett on the
staircase in Dunsany Castle
(1951). The original castle was
built here in 1403; St. Oliver
Plunkett was a member of the
family. County Meath.

This panoramic view of Wexford Town was taken from the tower of St. Peter's College in 1931. County Wexford.

*Opposite:*
Portrait of James Farrelly from the Wood of Allen (1929). County Kildare.

*See text, page 66*
'Kilkenny Old and New — a Fantasy' was how Father Browne captioned this remarkable picture in 1932. County Kilkenny.

'In the Shadow of the Press' at Longford (1935). County Longford.

*Cork*
*Waterford*
*Wexford*
*Tipperary*
*Limerick*
*Kerry*

Frank Browne was born in Cork in 1880 and often returned to his native city. His uncle, Robert Browne, was Bishop of Cloyne, his residence being beside the Cathedral of St. Colman in Cobh. Cork and Cobh, therefore, are given pride of place in this chapter.

Cork was a thriving metropolis during Frank's boyhood and — even more than today — was the hub of road, rail and shipping lines. The city buses were run by the Irish Omnibus Company. Narrow-gauge (as well as standard-gauge) railways covered most of Munster: the coaling of an ancient locomotive at Drimoleague Junction is given as a sample. Sailors, as well as their vessels, fascinated Father Browne: the portrait of an 'Old Salt' captures an expression that is full of far-away memories.

Frank spent many holidays in the Bishop's House at Cobh. It was his Uncle Robert, indeed, who bought him a first-class ticket for the maiden voyage of the *Titanic* in 1912. The photographer knew the captains of the two tenders, *Ireland* and *America*, which served the transatlantic liners calling to Queenstown in those days. As a result, he was able to photograph on board many of the White Star ships and Cunarders. The *Lusitania*, *Mauretania*, *Arabic*, *Olympic*, *Baltic*, *Caledonia* and *Laurentic* spring to mind. American, German, Dutch and Scandinavian liners were likewise photographed with passengers and crew. Emigrant ships were given a musical farewell as can be seen in one of these photographs of Cobh.

Frank's father, James Browne, used to go swimming at 6.30 every morning at Crosshaven. He died by drowning there in 1898. Frank's picture of a hardy Crosshaven swimmer, shown in this section, must have brought back poignant memories.

*Opposite:*
The traditional Bandon hooded cloak worn by Mrs. Murnane of Lisanisky (1941). County Cork.

It may have been a Bank Holiday, but Easter Monday
was still washing-day in Limerick in 1933. Limerick
City.

*Opposite:*
A section of the old walls of Waterford (1929). The
city was walled by the Danes before the end of the
tenth century but here we see remnants of the Anglo-
Norman fortifications which were built in the
thirteenth century. County Waterford.

'Golden youth of Tipperary'. The photographer visited Golden National School, near Cashel in 1929. County Tipperary.

'Shooters Shot' by the camera-man at Buttevant (1930). County Cork.

*Opposite:*
The Desmond Castle at Adare from the bridge over the River Maigue (1932). The strongly fortified keep was built in the early thirteenth century. County Limerick.

*Old Blarney Street (1934). Cork City.*

This photograph of Old Blarney Street in Cork City (1934) is remarkable because in many ways it might have been taken in any European city which dates back to the Middle Ages. The narrow thoroughfare, the central conduit for water and refuse, the lanterned street-lighting, the small houses: all of these combine to lend an air of antiquity to the whole.

Without the children, though, the picture would lose most of its impact. Compare this with the photograph of the Travelling People in County Mayo. Again, everyone has been asked to watch the camera. Again, all are in focus.

When he took this photograph, Father Browne must have recalled the days of his childhood in Cork. His family home was at Buxton Place in Sunday's Well, a much 'posher' district than this, but his family owned five houses in Blarney Street and had a tannery and flour-mill not far from this spot. The mansion of his grandfather (James Hegarty, who was Lord Mayor of Cork) stood quite near this spot until last year. With these associations, it is more than likely that the photographer actually knew the parents of the children he grouped so specifically in this shot.

'The Black and Tans' in full cry: not the infamous military force but the Tipperary hounds which gave them that name. Taken at Scarteen in 1933.

In still photography, moving images are tricky to record. They often take on forms and shapes that are not visible to the eye of the photographer at the time. The exposure can be much longer or shorter than the eye's perception. This timing translation has to be anticipated and, as much as possible, controlled. Given the technology available in 1933, we see here that Father Browne did his homework well.

The standpoint was well chosen, the ditch becoming a kind of stage across which the actors would eventually leap. A fast camera-setting was chosen to avoid blur. Two pitfalls were avoided. Had the dogs been all in the left half of the frame facing across the photograph, their movement would have appeared to have just started; if they were in the right half, with space behind them, their motion would have seemed completed. The photographer's timing was just right. His quick reflex action hit the one, brief, decisive moment that summed up the entire event.

The 'Black and Tans' in full cry (1933). County
Tipperary.

In Gibbs' workshop, Ballypatrick (1945). County
Tipperary.

*Opposite:*
Jenny Long offers advice on the tagging of boot-laces
at Pennywell (1937). Her father was one of the
hereditary 'rope-makers of Pennywell'. He was still
at work, aged seventy, when this picture was taken.
County Limerick.

Coaling the engine of the
Bantry train at Drimoleague
Junction in 1930. County
Cork.

'The Acrobat' was how Father Browne depicted this construction-worker in Limerick City (1937). Limerick City.

Hides for export at Waterford (1933). The port
continues to be one of the principal Irish exit-points
for the cattle trade. County Waterford.

*Opposite:*
'The Old Salt' at Blackrock (1934). Cork City.

An inspired view of St.
Colman's Cathedral (1934)
Cobh. County Cork.

The new suburb of Gurranabraher, taken from the
Cathedral Tower during the
St. Patrick's Day parade in
1934. Cork City.

*An inspired view of St. Colman's Cathedral, Cobh (1934)*

When ordinary photographers want to photograph a building they will normally begin by pointing their camera at it. Not so with the extraordinary Father Browne. He was always on the look-out for unusual angles. There are hundreds of examples of 'reflections' in his Collection, including a remarkble self-portrait looking into the placid water of a midland lake.

*See page 92*

Here we see St Colman's Cathedral in Cobh (1934), opportunely sighted after a rain-storm. It was not just by accident that he had his camera with him: he always had it with him. Of course he often had to rush his photographs when something fleeting but fascinating caught his attention. In this instance, he had plenty of time to compose his picture. No doubt he viewed the reflected spire from different distances before deciding on the best one.

Notice that he *did* want to include the shops in the background and *did* intend to keep them in focus. There are actually several terraces of houses above those shops before one rises to St. Colman's. The exclusion of these from the frame gives the impression that Cobh is a town on the flat, with a strange mirage to be seen by the mystical.

*The new suburb of Gurranabraher (1934)*

Vantage point. Father Browne frequently went to great lengths — and heights — to find one. Here he climbed the tower of St Mary's Cathedral in Cork to get an overview of the procession that took place on St Patrick's Day in 1934. A wide-angle lens supplemented the advantage gained.

*See page 93*

This is a historically interesting photograph because much of this part of Cork city has changed over the years. The building with the peculiar porch in the triangle formed by Bailey's Lane (now widened to Cathedral Road) and St Mary's Road used to be St Mary's Hall. It housed, at various times, a cinema, a savings bank and parochial offices. It once had its own small tower.

The Hall faced down Roman Street (Cathedral Street) with Shandon Street and Gerald Griffin Street runing west and east respectively. The latter is named after the author who became a Christian Brother.

The procession in 1934 was a big event in Cork. It marked the opening of the new housing-estate of Gurranabraher. Two hundred boy-scouts provided the colour-party for Bishop D. Cohalan who blessed the new suburb. One of those scouts was Walter McGrath of the *Cork Examiner* to whom I am indebted for the above information.

The trumpeter sounds the formal 'farewell' on the departure of a transatlantic liner in 1934. County Cork.

Patrick Street in 1932. Cork City.

Body of Bishop Robert Browne of Cloyne, the photographer's uncle (1935). Dr. Browne, a former President of Maynooth College, became bishop in 1894. He completed the building of St. Colman's Cathedral, Cobh and consecrated it in 1919. County Cork.

A summer scene at the sea-side resort of Tramore
(1933). County Waterford.

Richard Jones of the
Dolphin Swimming
Club, winner of the
Ocean Swimming Race
at Crosshaven, with
two members of the
organizing committee,
Munster Branch,
I.A.S.A. (1934).
County Cork.

'Miss Riley' nosing around Slea Head (1932). The
Blasket Islands can be seen on the sky-line. These
were still inhabited at the time but the islanders were
transferred to the mainland in 1953. County Kerry.

100    NORTH ● EAST ● **SOUTH** ● WEST

Mr. Donal O'Sullivan, Chairman of the Killarney
Urban District Council, pictured in the Macgil-
lycuddy Reeks near the Gap of Dunloe (1933).
County Kerry.

# WEST

*Clare*
*Galway*
*Sligo*
*Roscommon*
*Mayo*
*Leitrim*

You will notice, first, that we have put County Clare in the West of Ireland — where it rightly belongs. When Oliver Cromwell condemned the Irish 'to Hell or to Connacht', he meant west of the Shannon, including the stony fields of Clare. As a result of Cromwell's edict, there are more Catholics and fewer Protestants *per capita* in the west than elsewhere in Ireland. The Browne Collection reflects this fact. To illustrate the point, this section includes just one photograph of a Protestant church whereas there are four pictures of a Catholic nature. Let me hasten to repeat what I said in the introduction to the Northern photographs: Father Browne was a very convinced ecumenist and his Collection is catholic only with a small 'c'.

The Aran Islands, off County Galway, feature prominently in the Collection. I imagine that the photographer saw them as capable of being summed-up in their entirety via the camera's lens. The geographical restrictions imposed on the islanders' way-of-life meant that, within a small compass, everything was there for the taking. Father Browne, on his several visits, took photographs of people and places, people without places and places without people. Life, marriage and death; the sea as a way of life and a way of death; the land of stone where tough sheep produce tough wool for the weavers; children and adults — all come under tactful examination.

The West of Ireland is rightly famous for its scenery so here, more so than in any of the other sections, panoramic views of the countryside are given some prominence. In this regard, it is interesting to see that the photographer ignored those beauty-spots that are often seen on post-cards. He preferred to take views of little-known places such as Ballinafad in County Roscommon and Keshcorran in County Sligo.

*Opposite:*
The County Town of Ennis, seen through the south window of Friary Tower (1930). County Clare.

Compare this picture of children window-shopping in Galway City (1934) with the one of the ferry-boat on Upper Lough Erne (page 36). In both photographs Father Browne wanted to create an effect, not to take a portrait. He, himself, was obviously fascinated by that particular shop window. I imagine that he asked the by-passing children to stop and pose for him so as to add human interest and a sense of actuality.

The photograph contains so much detail that one could look at it for a long time. The *Connacht Tribune* (still extant, unlike some of the other publications seen here) catches the viewer's eye first, because that is where the children are looking. Nostalgic items, like the Swan Ink and the Irish Hospitals Sweepstake tickets at ten shillings each, will delight older viewers. What delights me is the amazing mixture of goods on display: the Infant of Prague beside the Summit Pens; the rosary beads beside the cigarettes; the sacred candles beside the movie magazine, and so on.

Without labouring the point, you might say that the whole image is 'so typically Irish'. If you look hard enough, you can see shamrocks, a Tara brooch, even the word, 'Irish'. At the same time there is something 'universal' about the photograph. You can find that word here too.

The O'Connell Monument in Ennis (1935). 'The Liberator' was M.P. for Clare, 1828-31. County Clare.

'Little Gaels' at Carrowcarew, near Maam (1925).
This is still an Irish-speaking area. County Galway.

*Opposite:*
Pilgrims climbing to the Mass Rock at Tubbercurry
(1932). Mass was celebrated out-of-doors here during
the Penal Days. County Sligo.

View of Dunavera Hill from Ballinafad (1936).
County Roscommon.

*Opposite:*
Panoramic view from the mouth of one of
Keshcorran Caves (1934). Legend tells us that the
famous High King of Ireland, Cormac Mac Airt, was
born here and nurtured by a she-wolf in one of the
caves. County Sligo.

*A wandering family near Urlar, County Mayo (1930)*

'The Gypsies' is what these people would have been called when Father Browne photographed them near Urlar in County Mayo in 1930. They are now more euphemistically known as the Travelling People. In other parts of the world they are said to be the descendants of ancient Egyptians or of the Romany folk of Central Europe. The Irish myth, which is possibly true in some cases, has it that they are descended from the Parthalonians, a pre-historic tribe which invaded Ireland about 500 B.C. The Gaelic name for Tallaght, County Dublin, is *Tamhleacht Muintir Parthalon*. Some historians maintain that it was from Tallaght that the present generation of travellers originated.

The mother of the family is seen here with seven of her children. Using a wide-angle lens, the photographer has managed to keep all the faces in focus. The curiosity, and a certain degree of wariness, is evident in the faces of the younger children. The older ones betray something more like resignation, despair or hopelessness. Distrust can be read in the face of the older girl on the left; shrewdness in the face of the boy on the right.

Despite her poverty, the mother seems to be coping. The photographer has included enough of the cart for us to tell that the family is in camp, not on the move. But perhaps they are just about to be told to move on.

*The weaver, at Onaght on Inishmore, the largest of the Aran Islands (1938)*

This photograph allows us to see Father Browne's attention to *lighting*. In the very early days of photography the main purpose of subject lighting was to provide enough illumination for a reasonably short exposure. Nowadays, faster films and lenses allow far more options, so that lighting can be used to express chosen aspects of the subject such as form, depth, texture, mood and detail. The way Father Browne grappled with the problems of indoor lighting in the 1930s was highly creative and individualistic.

*See page 112*

In this particular photograph the quality, direction, contrast, evenness and intensity of the lighting are combined in a masterly way. One immediately wonders where the light is actually coming from: is it natural or artificial? In fact Father Browne used a hard light beaming directly at the subject — not a practice to be advocated for amateurs because it has numerous pitfalls that can result in a phoney pose or a startled subject or a flared light coming straight back at the lens.

The photographer avoided these mishaps here, yet still provided sufficient light not only to illuminate the weaver but to show the unusual setting that so enhances the photograph. Notice that everything is in focus: the face, the bed, the picture of the Sacred Heart on the cottage wall.

The weaver at Onaght (1938). Aran Islands.

'A tinker tinkering' at Kiltoon (1930).
County Roscommon.

*Wedding at Oghil Church, Aran Islands. (1938)*

---

Father Browne was often called upon to photograph weddings. On this occasion, the bride is Mary Powell of Oghil. The groom is Patrick Hernon of Kilmurvey. Their big day was on 8th August 1938.

What is peculiar about this photograph is that, at first glance, you might think this is a funeral group rather than a wedding party. Looking longer, I think you will agree that beneath the fairly dour expressions there is a true feeling of happiness, of achievement.

Had there been steps outside the church, the photographer would doubtless have produced a more conventional picture with the guests in the background more visible. He had to cope with an untiered arrangement, yet he managed to make the most of the circumstances. Besides focussing on the couple in the centre himself, he enhanced this by having the people on either side look towards the bride and groom.

The photo is interesting, too, as a piece of social history. In Aran, like everywhere in rural Ireland at the time, people married rather late in life. I refrain from commenting more fully on this theme out of respect for the Hernon family. Suffice it to say that weddings, in one way, were taken for granted, a fact symbolized by the obtrusive cigarette right of centre.

*At the Mission Stall, Boyle, County Roscommon. (1948)*

---

This photograph, taken outside the Catholic Church in Boyle (1948), captures an essential ingredient of an Irish religious practice that has practially disappeared — the Parish Mission. From 1938 until he died in 1960, Father Browne was a member of the Jesuit Mission and Retreat staff. This explains how he managed to photograph every county in Ireland, as well as much of England, Scotland and Wales. A Parish Mission lasted for a fortnight: a week for the women and a week for the men. His main work did not begin until seven o'clock in the evening, although there would sometimes have been short sermons and devotions for school-children in the mornings. Father Browne introduced 'a Holy Half-Hour' for children in Castlewellan, County Down, in 1938. In the afternoons, if there was no personal counselling to be done, he would be out and about with his camera.

*See page 116*

I am reliably informed that, as a preacher, he did not adopt the 'fire and brimstone' approach that was so prevalent in his day. He believed in bringing people to the love of God, not to the fear of God.

We can be sure, too, that he inculcated ecumenical ideals long before they became the accepted norm. In 1960, Lord Nugent wrote an obituary in the *Irish Guards Association Journal*. One sentence reads: 'Everyone in the Battalion, officer or man, Catholic or Protestant, loved and respected Father Browne and he had great influence for good.'

Wedding at Oghil Church on 8th August, 1938. The
bride is Mary Powell of Oghil; the bridegroom is
Patrick Hernon of Kilmurvey. Aran Islands.

At the Mission Stall during the
Jesuit Mission, Boyle (1948).
County Roscommon.

The Corpus Christi procession at
Tubbercurry (1932). County Sligo.

On the road near Frenchpark
(1934). County Roscommon.

'Permanent Way — Permanent Wave' was Father Browne's caption for this photograph taken in Loughrea in 1950. County Galway.

The silver screen brings
the Caribbean to
Athenry in 1933.
County Galway.

'Curiosity' was how Fr. Browne entitled this study of a small boy examining a knife-sharpener (1933). County Galway.

## Portrait of an old man at Crossmolina, County Mayo (1938)

*See page 122*

An example of Father Browne's use of wide aperture (f/2) camera-setting. The shallow depth of field concentrates our interest on the weather-beaten face. The photographer has thus placed the emphasis where he wanted it to be. The out-of-focus background simply suggests an environment; it does not show details that clutter or confuse. Minimising the depth of field with a wide aperture meant that Father Browne had to be really accurate with his focussing because there was little latitude for error.

If, on the other hand, the photographer had chosen the greatest possible depth of field in this instance, his picture would have contained more information. It can be argued that this would have been more 'natural', more like seeing the actual subject, leaving the viewer to decide what to concentrate on rather than being dictated to by Father Browne.

The argument, in essence, boils down to the question: do you resent being dictated to by a *great* photographer? Father Browne mastered his craft and, by comparing this picture with most of the others in this book, you will see that he chose his criteria carefully. It is only rarely that he dictates. His dictation is appropriate.

One hardly needs to add that the figure in the photograph is deliberately off-centre. Symmetry is boring. Father Browne was no bore.

## Interior, Church of Ireland Cathedral of St Nicholas, Galway (1932)

*See page 125*

Father Browne was particularly adept at photographing the interiors of churches and cathedrals. We know from the articles he wrote for *The Kodak Magazine* in the 1930s that he went to considerable trouble in achieving his desired effect. As every amateur photographer knows, it is difficult to photograph the inside of a large building which has windows. Usually, there will be excessive contrast between the bright areas near the windows and the darker parts of the building. Father Browne solved this problem by using supplementary artificial light combined with existing daylight. (Incidentally, he had tried to photograph some English cathedrals after dark, using only artificial lights, but found the results unsatisfactory due to their uneven quality).

Here in Galway we see a splendid example of an evenly-lit interior. Portable lamps have been placed in such a way that there are no obtrusive reflections. Indeed the overall effect is so perfect that it is hard to credit that artificial light has been used at all. You will notice, too, that the upper details of the image are as brightly lit (with 'bounced' light to avoid harshness) as the lower portions. The overall result is that a dimly-lit interior seems to have been evenly painted with light.

Father Browne's guide at Stonefield, near Erris Head (1935). County Mayo.

*Opposite:*
A study of an old man at Crossmolina (1938). County Mayo.

On the life-boat, leaving
Inishmaan (1938). Aran
Islands.

In Providence Woollen Mills,
Foxford (1938). County
Mayo.

Battle trophies on display in
St. Nicholas' Cathedral,
Galway (1932). Galway City.

Sisters. Outside her cottage home, near Drumshanbo (1933). County Leitrim.

A stroll on Inisheer in 1938. Aran Islands.